AF430528

Preface

This is the preterm birthing story
of Lexington Wade,
written by his Mother

If you are interested in a
similar personalized creation
and would like our help please contact
us at TheEarlyBearBook@gmail.com

Dedication

**Dedicated to Lexington Wade,
with a special thank you to
his eldest Aunt Ceterra,
for whom I am forever greatful.**

The Bear Family had a big party to celebrate the Baby Bear.

Their hearts were so full that they planned and decorated with great care.

LEX
X

Two days before Christmas was
his original birth date.

Some arrive early while others are late.
Yet, each baby is an incredible blessing,
at any rate.

One morning Mother Bear had a
tummy ache.

She quickly realized she had a
few phone calls to make.

After calling Granny, Baby Bear's Aunt and
Father Bear with the news of feeling ill.

Mother Bear prayed while traveling to the
Hospital down Bearyhill.

HOSPITAL

The Baby Bear's Aunt arrived and
called Father Bear to tell him Mother
Bear was indeed sickly.

Babies can't remain safe in sick Mommies
so they must be moved quickly!

The Baby Bear was tiny and had to
stay in the hospital longer.

Nurses and Doctors cared for
him until he became stronger.

N.I.C.U

Mother and Father Bear visited the
Early Baby Bear during his hospital stay.

They even brought milk from home each
and every day.

HOSPITAL

For weeks the Early Baby Bear lived
with the other early bears
in the hospital.

Yet, he remained strong and couragous
with no signs of whittle.

N.I.C.U

The entire Bear Family prayed each day
for the Early Bear's release.

The Nurse called saying the Baby Bear
was ready to go home and it
gave them great peace.

1984